THE EVENING ENTERTAINMENT

MATTHEW PAUL
THE EVENING ENTERTAINMENT

 **EYEWEAR** PUBLISHING

First published in 2017
by Eyewear Publishing Ltd
Suite 333, 19-21 Crawford Street
Marylebone, London w1h 1pj
United Kingdom

Cover design and typeset by Edwin Smet
Author photograph by Lyn Paul
Printed in England by TJ International Ltd, Padstow, Cornwall

The right of Matthew Paul to be identified as author of
this work has been asserted in accordance with section 77
of the Copyright, Designs and Patents Act 1988
ISBN 978-1-911335-64-1

*Eyewear wishes to thank Jonathan Wonham for his
generous patronage of our press.*

WWW.EYEWEARPUBLISHING.COM

For Lyn

MATTHEW PAUL
was born in New Malden, Surrey,
in 1966, read Philosophy at the University of Ulster,
and lives and works on the outskirts of London. He was
shortlisted for the Poetry School/Pighog Press pamphlet
competition 2013, and has had his poems published in a
variety of publications, including *Butcher's Dog*, *Magma*,
Nth Position, *Poetry Ireland Review*, *The Rialto*, and *The Best
New British and Irish Poets* for both 2016 and 2017 (Eyewear
Publishing), and is a participant on the Poetry Business
Writing School programme 2017/2018. He is the author
of two collections of haiku – *The Regulars* (2006) and *The
Lammas Lands* (2015) – and co-writer/editor (with John
Barlow) of *Wing Beats: British Birds in Haiku* (2008), all
published by Snapshot Press. He co-edits
Presence haiku journal and has contributed
to *The Guardian*'s 'Country Diary'
column.

TABLE OF CONTENTS

1

HIGH WIRE — 10

SWALLOWING THE TOAD — 11

THE TOXTON TORCHERS — 12

THE BOATING LAKE — 13

JACOB AND THE ANGEL — 14

SCARLETT'S PLACE — 15

RIGMAROLE — 16

A DELEGATION FROM THE SHIRES PETITIONS THE MINISTER
WITHOUT PORTFOLIO — 17

THE SCHLIEFFEN PLAN — 18

THE SKIP — 19

THE KITCHEN GARDEN — 20

THE LOCUM DENTAL HYGIENIST — 21

THE LEAVING DO — 22

STOWAWAY — 23

EX — 24

THE PASSING WINTER — 25

HOP PICKING — 27

TAKING CONTROL — 28

THE BLUE COAST BLUES — 29

CLEMENTINES — 30

MRS PEABODY — 31

THE STONES AT REDLANDS — 32

THE HENGIST MEN — 33

DOWN CREAMERY LANE — 34

JUNIPER CHILD — 35

AMERICANO — 36

SWALLOWTAILS — 37

SIX ITEMS OR FEWER — 38

THE SURFERS OF ROCK-A-NORE — 39

2

HALF BOARD AT THE ALUM SANDS HOTEL — 42
COLUMBIA PARK — 43
THE CHIMPS — 44
APING CHEETA — 45
SANDCASTLING — 46
RUNNERS-UP — 47
THE WINTER OF DISCONTENT — 48
MANTRA — 49
CHALK — 50
THE TRIUMPH OF SYLVESTER CLARKE — 51
HEREDITY — 52
NUMANOID — 53
KING FOR A DAY — 54
FIRST DIGS — 55
ISOSCELES — 56
KINGSTON — 57
PIETÀ — 58
DUCKWALKING IN WEST BERLIN — 59
THE GREAT STORM — 60
DONNY GILLIGAN THE LAB TECHNICIAN — 61
RASHARKIN — 63
POSTCARDS TO PORT — 64
SENSATIONAL HUMAN CANNONBALL — 65

3

SCARECROW — 68
THE SLEEPER — 69
VINYL — 70
SUNDAY AT THE OVAL WITH DAD — 71
HEADGEAR — 72
THE SIDECAR — 73
BRITISH SUMMER TIME'S END — 74
THE D WORD — 75
THE SEWING KIT — 76
QUEEN QUEENIE — 77

NOTES — 79
ACKNOWLEDGEMENTS — 81

1

HIGH WIRE

On a good day, which, by the sunrays
tripping through the cumulus, this could be,
when my toes reach along and my heel
presses down to finish the foothold,
my thoughts sometimes wander
to the possibilities of lunch
 – fine dining at La Pesca with the crew,
or the remnants of yesterday's fennel risotto –
and how I ought to buy a new pair
of red-and-white wire-walking shoes,
custom-made in Milan; but today,
when I step out from the small door
on the thirty-first storey's breeze-block roof
and balance upon the beautiful tautness
stretching my mind, I sense
after just my seventh tread,
and know for definite on the eighth,
that three-quarters of the way to the other side
the banshee winds which scrape my face
would send me plunging like a gannet;
so I devour consciousness
as if it's the last and greatest meal of my life,
arch my toes upwards
and ghost the eight paces backwards
to a frosted shot glass of grappa.

SWALLOWING THE TOAD

And I well remember the time, but was not an eye-witness to the fact
(though numbers of persons were) when a quack at this village ate a toad
to make the country people stare; afterwards he drank oil.
– Gilbert White, *The Natural History of Selborne*, 1789

Was it still alive? Well, while that man
of medicine crunched the first of its fore feet
in the midsummer evening sunshine
burnishing the priory pond, its copper eyes
blinked not once but thrice. They say
that, just like us, toads eventually return
to the waters where they were spawned.
This noble chap had had his nuptial pads
wrestled from amplexus; yes, wrenched off
the partner he'd royally piggybacked
since the solstice. Why did I let it happen?
I had no authority with which to intervene.
Yet I was the only witness who flinched
when the last of his bull head disappeared.

THE TOXTON TORCHERS

Still their identities are secret. Let's call them Gary and Glyn,
names which are popular then, at the Sixties' fag-end.
This nit-locked pair of toe-rags, seeking alms box and plate,
enter St Joe's via its sacristy, find nothing of value
and burn down the sanctuary like proper East End heavies.

They're not discerning: any place of worship will do –
in the next few weeks, Our Lady Star of the Sea, St Anne's,
the Kingdom Hall and the new St Margaret's all go up in flames.
It's when they smash collection boxes in All Souls that it ends:
old Reverend Carew and his nimble curate get straight on the blower
to the Law, who tip up in Black Marias at *Z-Cars* speed.

Gary blames it all on gormless Glyn. Brought before the Bench,
their eyes light up like matches as they detail every deed:
how in the new church they hadn't the heart to torch the tapestries
as so much effort had been put into them, most by Gary's nan.

THE BOATING LAKE

Plying a pedalo, the sole customer frowns
beneath his fringe because the coastal breeze
has saved up its breath for a right good go
at billowing into storm mode. Over the swell,
he can't hear the teenage attendant, who really
doesn't want a drowning on her shift; but our man
coxed for Leander in his youth so he steers
an impeccable course through the tempest
to step triumphantly from craft to shore
in as fluent a movement as the pitch-perfect poise
of a maverick Olympic yachtsman.

JACOB AND THE ANGEL

Genesis 32 : 24–30

I can't say either of us truly found our groove.
We exhausted our entire repertoires of moves:
pile drivers, headbutts, a hangman hold, a splash;
nelsons both half and full, the kamikaze crash...
For grapple connoisseurs, it must've been *some* bout.
I like to believe we cancelled each other out.
He dodged my Boston crab and tried to wallop me
with a smash; then his short-arm scissors collared me.
I'm not ashamed to say I howled like a gibbon –
but at *no point* did I think about submission.
Neither did he; built, as he was, like Apollo.
He reeled from my tomahawk chop, which I followed
with the death lock I'd been taught by a Seminole.
It was God's turn to bawl. We tussled for my soul.

SCARLETT'S PLACE

When Scarlett pulls on
Spiderman gloves
and Mister Spock ears
she's in her box
where no-one can disturb her
as she plays an organ with one hand
and scribbles in circles
with magenta crayon
with the other
until her music and picture
both somewhat resemble
an unopened punnet
of semi-furred strawberries
flown in from California.

RIGMAROLE

If you should call me 'malcontent,
pen-pushing pawn of government',

sat as I am, without cushion,
in the cloistered scriptorium,

enriching the codex, stating
my pitch and fervour, by scraping

off forebears' illegible screed,
replaced with gold-leaf filigree,

then you might say 'it's rigmarole,
raggedy tattling, ragman roll',

that I incise onto vellum,
for *Edwardus, rex Anglorum*.

Every recto and verso glows;
soft sun on an Eleanor cross.

It's now I make the retching sign
for a Gospel that's forbidden.

Men can be blinded for as much.
The crows in westward flight at dusk

crack the silence, end my labour.
I seek, therefore, our Saviour.

A DELEGATION FROM THE SHIRES PETITIONS THE MINISTER WITHOUT PORTFOLIO

Once the whizz-kid civil servants have faffed
about and the Minister's fully briefed
as to whom he's meeting today and why,
the county councillors only have time –
less than fifteen enervating minutes –
to get across, with verve, three killer points,
like Ruritanian ambassadors
at Court, desperate to ferret out favours.
First, they must permit him to perorate,
as if his remit is to educate
yokel politicians in Whitehall ways.
After, they opine that they made their case
rather well; discerning, from a phrase he
used, a pledge of cash. Now they wait and see.

THE SCHLIEFFEN PLAN

The last to leave, she tanks
    through the open plan, neon-lit
between the workstation banks,
    to breach the Secretariat

and palm-push the portholed
    door to the office of *Herr Direktor*
whose hulking desk is silhouetted
    by the hunter's moon which pours

its light upon tomorrow's date
    displayed by the rotary numbers
of his fondly-remembered late
    father's woodblock perpetual calendar.

THE SKIP

In no time after arrival that morning
at number nine, it was full to overflowing
with everyone else's shite, from all along

Tennyson Terrace. I'd itched to stay up late,
well past my bedtime, to watch the neighbours nip out
by moonlight and deposit the usual tat:

mattresses stained with a Turin shroud of spunk;
an analogue telly that would break a man's back
if he lugged it on his own; three-legged chairs, Coke

cans, clotted condoms; miscellaneous crap.
But what no-one expected underneath the heap,
when at last they carted it off to the tip,

was a head- and limb-less Caucasian man,
whose identity the Police would never learn,
in bloat stage; a gutful of maggoty churn.

I curse like a barrow boy for missing my turn.

THE KITCHEN GARDEN

On Capability Brown's last visit
to this well-temperèd chalkland estate,
he plumped for action instead of advice:
training espaliers of local pears,

which would otherwise have become extinct,
against ev'ry venerable wall of brick –
'for market opportunities', he said,
and focused eyes on an artichoke head

whose outer bracts formed interlaced patterns
around the heart's delirious embrace,
aubergine-veined chroma of grey–jade green.
He claimed it resembled 'a scarecrow's brain'.

Unaccountably, he bricked up the arch,
to dead-end our last remaining path;
so now unscaleable walls enclose us,
in God's own country's *Hortus conclusus*.

THE LOCUM DENTAL HYGIENIST

describes her time
in Abu Dhabi, where
the air-conditioning

was 'so damned high'
that she had to wear tights
and a cardigan every day;

but she never tired
of the chicory skies
on the drive into work

or the chance to remark
to all of her regulars,
'Turned out nice again'.

THE LEAVING DO

You're already ancient history:
for months you've been demob-happy
and senior management have less and less often
invited you to meetings or solicited your view;
so here you are yet again – though this time
unexpectedly for *your* turn – in the Fox and Hounds,
where your deputy reserved an area from 5pm:
you emailed every name in the corporate address book,
plus a few old faces who managed to escape before you;
anyone, basically, who might give a toss. After three jolly
Happy Hours, on an unknown but quaffable brand of fizz,
there's a fair-sized turn-out considering it's a school night.
Your team are patently delighted to be seeing you off,
though most dissemble from politeness. Some folk say
you're going because you don't think they're good enough;
pronounce at the bar that you've been over-promoted.
One or two seem genuinely pleased to see you succeed.
Thus the evening develops into *This is Your Life*:
each vodka brings retirees looking so much chirpier
than before they left, and colleagues you've not seen
for yonks, fully reminding you why. That's when
Vivienne from Finance appears at your elbow
and wells up unstoppably, as she'll miss you 'like mad',
and you never, *ever*, even guessed.

STOWAWAY

What did he dream it would be like here, among us,
on an East Sheen avenue's crab-appled pavements?
From the kwanza banknotes they find on his person,
the Police not unreasonably think he's Angolan;
indeed, a plane from Luanda flew right over
that morning; but a sim card in his boxers proves,
in fact, he's Jose Pássaro from Mozambique.
Trembling, hypothermic, frostbitten, hypoxic,
he's wearing on his top half only a short-sleeve,
last-season United away-shirt and a glove.
Unconscious, his grasp loosens from the landing gear...
Residents lament the Harvest Sunday scatter
of entrails on their drives. Jose's next of kin are
being informed. The Council clear away the gore.

EX

Beware his mockney patter – scattering aitches
like soggy lettuce from a Friday-night kebab –
and the soiled punchlines to his skunk-infused gags
that nobody, including him, ever catches.

Everywhere – my Uncle Peregrine's bungalow
down a stitchwort-embroidered lane near Pevensey;
your sister's civil partnership ceremony
in a Stuart mansion in Breckland – that we go,

we never escape his rants, even during sex:
always lurking in the dark is his monstrous laugh,
as if he can pick up where he thinks he left off,
scavenger–predator, *Tyrannosaurus rex*.

THE PASSING WINTER

'London ravens' were easily identified at rabbit warrens in the country
by the dirty brown of their plumage, compared with the jet-black of the
country ravens, due to their wallowing in the dirt when getting their food.
– R.S.R. Fitter, *London's Natural History*, 1945.

It's the opposite of dog days:
snow that wasn't forecast to fall
still flurries along the byways

like a borough councillor's drawl.
A freeze and I'll come a cropper.
The central heating makes me ill.

It isn't clear from the clobber
she carries on her back what sport
she plays (even why she bothers),

but my upstairs neighbour-of-sorts
never passes up a morning
to fetch herself out of the flats.

Upon the weather vane, turning
on the Guildhall's red-brick steeple
in a sky whose pink is draining

away, a magpie perches, still
as a bronze. Into the hawthorn
hedges, which demarcate the hill,

a dog fox leaps with elision,
pausing to behold like he's
the King of Surbiton Lagoon,

where a synchronised unkindness
of dust-brown ravens stops to drink
on its return from greensand fields.

There's too much time for me to think.
I focus my jumbled-up gaze
on what assembles in a blink:
an apple tree filling with jays.

HOP PICKING

You'd see them gossiping in their curlers
every dusk, outside the Red Cow, puffing
away on fags: gangs of evacuees
from London. Whenever the Luftwaffe
flew over, they'd dive into a hedgerow
while we carried on working rewardless.
But when the doodlebugs started, we too
hid. Once, we watched from our hopper huts
some Spitfires shoot one into a blaze
and spin, straight down among Billy Read's fields,
where his herd of pedigree Red Polls grazed:
barrel became brisket, and hip yielded
sirloin; thurl furnished rump, while withers
bore chuck. We all wailed for our fathers.

TAKING CONTROL

In Dior frock and pearls, Lisa Blatch stoops
to board the BOAC flying boat that's moored
in Southampton Water – followed, a breath behind,

by dinner-jacketed Stuart, her husband,
who flew one throughout the evacuation
from Crete, as he's repeatedly retold Lisa

by the time they've sunk several Manhattans each,
before dinner, somewhere over Spain.
The long haul to Jo'burg will take four days.

That the stewardess insists on calling Stuart
'Group Captain' despite his demob
only increases Lisa's sense of pique.

In her debutante days, big-game hunting
in the Orange Free State was not quite how
she'd envisaged spending her honeymoon.

Stuart is all for asking the Captain
if he can take the controls for old times' sake.
Lisa sighs and wishes him 'Bon Voyage'.

THE BLUE COAST BLUES

The merriment that day was just as you remember:
at the sea-terrace windows, your knowing, debonair
parents, Stuart and Lisa Blatch, brandy and soda

in hand, and all your siblings, ranging widely in age.
Processions of incoming planes strobe the Baie des Anges.
Professor Longhair is blaring out. He's all the rage.

The walls are deckchair-striped in Rococo pink and blue.
Outside, from the beach, someone photographs the tableau,
to be conjured into a jigsaw for you to do

when you furnish your own first home. You're the eldest boy,
intent upon bathing. Turquoise combers froth away.
Gendarmes with kid-gloves boss the Promenade des Anglais.

The snow-capped massif parasols your features as you're
snoozing at the beach. You let your sloshing dreams take their
course, through the sandy sediment of the night before.

CLEMENTINES

From the clam shell palette,
    his brush lifts coral onto a plate,
where he spits a tarry, liquorice hackle
    threaded by strands of saffron tobacco:
saliva bubbles slowly off his tongue,
    to thicken the water like tempera.
He paints his daughter's portrait
    from pharmaceutical memory,
with the same arms-akimbo pose
    that he, himself, perfected as a child.
That he retains a clear image of her,
    and pays as much attention to the gloss
of the background clementines
    clustered in a porcelain bowl,
can't, for a moment, paint over
    his white-hot recollection
of premature severance and pain.

MRS PEABODY

was the taciturn lady from number forty-two
who everyone referred to as 'the strongwoman,
married to an acrobat'. She could: tear into quarters

two telephone-directories at once; lift above her head
baby-oiled heavyweight boxer Crusher Bates
and cradle him in her arms like a newborn; and lull

a hefty tug-of-war team into thinking they were
winning, then, with just one pull, send them piling
into a heap, like an eight-legged pantomime horse.

She's there in the photo of Dawn's fifth birthday party
in 1965, at the family home in Vale Road, directly
behind the gap-toothed birthday-girl's latest best friend:

bee-hived, in a Paisley-patterned house-coat, smiling.

THE STONES AT REDLANDS

on 'Sunshine' acid
chance upon cows being milked
up Sheepwash Lane –
see how the sunlit milk pours
endlessly, endlessly, into the pail...

THE HENGIST MEN

play just one gig, at Middle Earth, with The Soft Machine
    and Arthur Brown, before upping sticks from town
to get their shit together. Maybe it's the endless
    supply of acid, but the long afternoons are always
sunny as they wander the Wessex heartlands
    in Jake's Morris Traveller. Swallows weave contrails
between the Avebury stones. At the top of Bredon
    one fondant dawn, the counties spread below them
cohere. They kayak the Kennet; mirroring their drift
    from psychedelia to free-form folk–jazz–rock,
culminating in David's fifteen-minute arrangement
    of 'The Banks of Green Willow'. At Marlborough,
they gawp at a spectral duck nesting in an oak;
    instantly, Dick riffs the first few licks of what becomes
their best-known track, 'Mandarin Girl', a by-word
    for pastoral indulgence. With mixed success, they each
go solo in the Seventies, and change their junk
    with the coke-cocked times, before a painful reunion,
in a Bronze Age barrow, on the eve of Punk.

DOWN CREAMERY LANE

If you leant for a while on the Long Field fence,
the leader of the Friesians, slinging
her bathroom-light-cord tail at the blowflies,
would dander over and check you out
with a face that's wholly unreadable.
Then all the herd would buffet and bash
to get a good squiz, as if they'd cornered
the runtiest kid in the playground.
Would they smile? Laugh? You'd look
from cow to cow, size up their eyes'
resemblance to dark-chocolate truffles.
But if you wallowed in a communing-
with-creatures glow, they'd silently turn tail,
without an obvious signal from any of them.
And as if by appointment, you'd spy
an upturned bicycle, one wheel spinning
toward your finger's most delicate touch.

JUNIPER CHILD

The masks and shakers were removed just once
from their case, for an ad hoc performance

that served as a lament for the child
who never was: his body was barrowed

from Great Monk Wood – bundles of juniper
kindling gathered up by an unknown pair

of hands, hired for the apple harvest.
His outsized head was moulded from compost;

his porcelain face had redcurrant eyes,
a windfall Worcester Pearmain for a nose.

The ceaseless shuffling of a scold of jays
loosed downpours of acorns at Martinmas –

their plumage banished the child's landlock.
His torso ignited when lightning struck.

The masks and shakers were again locked up.
The child's grave isn't marked on the map.

AMERICANO

The gastronaut
can't resist a zebra spider
this Advent morning

(it's the way it hangs
from the station rafters
at a gulpable height);

pushes the door
of the platform snack-bar
and orders a regular

black Americano
to wash down
a couple of legs

awkwardly lodged,
like blackberry pips,
between her teeth.

SWALLOWTAILS

At night they strip the remnants of a grapefruit lobbed aside
by bikers rolling through to Tennessee. You're here
because you're a collector, bearing your great-uncle Theo's
collapsible net. As the passenger in a monster SUV,
hired for the day from a dicey lot in downtown Winston-Salem,
you felt it surf up Highway 421 towards the Blue Ridge Parkway,
where the pine heat seeps in despite the windows being closed
for the air-con. Now you've stopped at an overlook
near Blowing Rock, beside a field full of life. The only sounds
in the thin August air are the ticks of the cooling engine.
The torchlight on your head is dimmed to the ideal pitch.
The grass springs back behind your heels. You pigeon-step.
You hold back a sneeze. You collect. First, the Giant Swallowtails,
vanilla and black, their tails shadowed on your shoes; then
you up your game, to the Pipevines and Eastern Tigers. You
couldn't care less what else you net in passing. You head
for Asheville. Storm clouds shake loose over Grandfather Mountain.
A stag irrupts into the headlights' glare; its antlers and sinews
freeze-framed, evading the hood by the merest nip, to tear
through lightning the greenest way back home. And on you collect,
like you're coveting the final side plate of a Meissen dinner service
hatched for Augustus the Strong in an edition of one. You collect.

> evening heat
> the unseen sapsucker
> drums five times

SIX ITEMS OR FEWER

The bloke at the check-out
tells the listening cashier

he's the last of his family-line;
talks about his sweet tooth,

how he really mustn't buy
a Christmas pud this year,

as there will only be him
to slather it in whisky,

smear on clotted cream
and all too slowly eat it.

THE SURFERS OF ROCK-A-NORE

all pulled sickies to come paddling-up here,
behind the village of ink-black net sheds
this bleak Monday morning, carving the swell
through another 'yellow' weather warning
of westerlies whistling in from Greenland,
on chops and bombs the colour of sea kale.

We lean on the railings between which
the best surfer clambers to pad back round
again after each wipe-out, his jet hair
tasselling down his wetsuit like the blades
of dead men's laces. The long leash slackens
from ankle to board. He cutbacks thin air.

Along their makeshift beach, turnstones bicker
over mussels; skedaddling clockwork toys
in summer-plumage camouflage. In such
blustering, they're reassuringly tame,
oblivious to the gnarly breakers
cymballing at their feet within our reach.

The surfers flounder in the undertow,
yet somehow attract a sizeable crowd
fixating on fortitude, amplify
protestations of happiness, and ride
a perfect shorey into whitewater,
petering out under cross-Channel sky.

2

HALF BOARD AT THE ALUM SANDS HOTEL

We zigzag down to the beach, where we deck our castles
    with miniature Scottish flags and bury each other right up to the neck.

Bursts of the *Radio 1 Roadshow* from scattered transistors
    mix with the shrieks of generations jumping the breakers.

Between dips, we pig ourselves sick on cheese-and-pickle rolls
    and homemade rock-cakes moistened by tea from a tartan thermos.

At the hotel, there's just enough time for ping-pong
    over a sagging net in the basement Games Room

before Mum makes us change into shirts and corduroys for dinner.
    It's either orange juice or grapefruit for starters. The main course

is a roast with croquette potatoes and peas, topped off
    by sherry trifle and Dad's urbane request for the cheeseboard.

The evening entertainment – one man and his Casio keyboard
    piping 'Tie a Yellow Ribbon' – gets Mum and Dad jiving.

We straw-suck the dregs from our glasses of cider.
    Longer than a week would be murder.

COLUMBIA PARK

All that drizzly summer, cheeking 'Parkie'
with language we wouldn't use at home
became routine, but he never replied in kind;
instead he kept our ball when he could grab it.
Kickabouts arose with many-a-side:
we brothers against the Shackletons
and any other boys who fancied a game.

Some unleashed mongrel inevitably tore about
to stab its glue-coloured teeth in the innards,
not letting go until the owner caught it up
and smacked it on the nose. By the end of August,
the nettles were strewn with misshapen footballs,
each one holding, in the flaky leather's folds,
a mazy dribble of moss-lined rain.

THE CHIMPS

Slapping hands and honking, we race
from sea lions to the ape house,
where Tizer orangutans pace.

But one among us nine-year-olds
watches alone; not with Mr Dodds,
nor any other adult or kids:

Helen Crawshaw, who we all say reeks
of Brussels sprout farts, by golly looks
the spit of Lizzie Dripping; and talks

just like her too. Chimpanzees take turns
to lob chunky, bituminous turds
through the narrow gaps between the bars,

full flush into the face of Helen,
who doesn't budge, but takes it on the chin,
longer than anyone else would grin

and bear it. Mr Dodds yanks her frame
from the chimps' redoubtable aim
and shepherds her back the way we came.

APING CHEETA

My brothers and I watch Tarzan tub-thump
his vulcanized chest and bug-eyedly rip
his call through the jungle to plant-trampling
elephants. Cheeta, like us, starts jumping
as quicksand envelops our hero's feet:
without a liana to clasp, Tarzan's right
in it up to his loin-cloth. Just in time,
two elephants join their trunks around him.
Cheeta leaps and capers euphorically.
Tarzan's levered out before safari-
suited baddies can shove his head under.
We play the scene straight after – I'm Cheeta:
my whooping draws Dad downstairs to make us
desist, and roll his eyes the way he does.

SANDCASTLING

A spaniel springs off its leash.
With panoptical zooming,
we take in the width of the beach:

there's charms of kids performing
Cruyff-turns for fun. 'Do what you
want, but come if you're coming,'

shouts a girl who has to go.
We mould castles in buckets
and moats in the undertow.

Even as we dig deep cuts,
half by hand, they're washed away.
Where the beef of our spade bites,

the sand's as gloopy as clay-
slip, undermines the ramparts
and parapets completely

with unstaunchable movements,
takes the castle's hollowed keep
and snaffles the battlements,
lapped by sun, in one fell swoop.

RUNNERS-UP

You wouldn't guess from looking at the photo
which player in the sky-blue kitted team –
six of whom stand upright, with arms crossed,
behind the hunkering other five –
is destined within weeks to die
while the rest transfer to secondary school.

Nor would you pick me out, blond
and mop-topped as I am then, squinting
beside perma-grinning Robert Scott.
It's the last time I see him. He chases
his family's schnauzer round the garden, not clocking
that the door of their new conservatory's shut –

and charges straight through, headfirst,
to be floored like a punctured football.

THE WINTER OF DISCONTENT

Snow on the bins. Dad's poaching herrings in milk again.
The cat's going Radio Rental. Mum sings. Wogan
chunters over 'Beautiful Noise'. My unwashed noggin

in the bathroom mirror looks the colour of clay creeks
feeding the four-mile-wide Thames estuary which keeps
our shore from Kent. We take it all for granted that each

morning will start like this: the pouring of PG Tips
from a sage-green Beryl teapot into matching cups;
the serving-up by spatula of lard-fried doorsteps

culled from yesterday's bloomer, tiger-striped tomatoes,
Co-op liver sausage and streaky bacon, for those
of our five-strong clan who really can't abide kippers.

MANTRA

The number 213 and the redness of its rear
are all I see of the disappearing bus, before
another one slips the ropes of the hill,
heaving with posh kids from a different school,
with stripier blazers and caps. I find half a seat
upstairs, right at the back in the smokiest part,
next to a bloke whose grumbling guts doo-wop
like one-hit wonders on *Top of the Pops*.

I catch a glimpse through a steamed-up window –
where someone's finger-drawn a cock and arrow –
of the just-mown triangle of Plough Green
and its tadpoled pond in which the woman
who delivered meals-on-wheels with my mum
drowned herself one Christmas Day. Then we come
to the bridge with its famous mantra daubed
high in white, reeking of the grown-ups' world:

SEXY WOMAN I LOVE YOU MANHOOD.

CHALK

Wobbling my orange racer,
I follow a trail of white-chalked
arrows around to Highdown,
at the Barrow Hill end of which
lies bramble-tangled rough ground
– for rough boys and girls –
overlooking the grandstand
at Epsom Downs. My curiosity
clabbers into sour vexation.
There's no solution to the mystery.
    I make my way back seething,
and kick the side-gate open
with such a wallop that Dad,
from his rhubarb patch,
yells, 'Pack it in!'
    Days later, up Perry How,
I find and challenge the screever,
a boy about my age, who's chalking
another trail, in Man. City blue.
When I ask him why, he smirks –
as if I'm a right dolt for being
so irritable, so typically thirteen.

THE TRIUMPH OF SYLVESTER CLARKE

The first day's play centred around the hostile bowling of Clarke...
— Wisden Cricketers' Almanack, 1981

It's a rare full house, mostly comprised of coach-loads down from the Ridings. When the umpires and Surrey dawdle to the middle, the monkey-whoops begin. The recipient, Sylvester Theophilus Clarke, 'barrel-chested Barbadian', shows no reaction as he marks out his run-up. But there's a menace in his step as he limbers in, to louder chants, and hurls a ball-as-missile beamer at tremendous pace, veering over the opener, Bill Athey, and the 'keeper, for four wides. The Yorks. fans' jeers are deafening. Athey isn't quite so sanguine. Clarke's deliveries are viciously varied; brilliance finding its mojo.

And then Boycott's on strike, all fresh, imperial-white wrist-bands and chewing-gum; proprietarily steps forward to prod invisible bumps with his bat and survey the field. Having leg-glanced Jackman for four, he's getting his eye in. But Clarke rumbles up like a jouster: the first ball's a bouncer; ricochets off the pitch to smack Boycott's unprotected shoulder. The whole ground knows what's coming next: through the gap beneath Boycott's bat, the fastest, in-swinging yorker slap-banging plumb against his pads. As umpire Alley raises his finger, a humbling instant of utmost distillation hangs . . .

Clarke goes on to plunder wickets on two rebel tours of apartheid South Africa, to safeguard his future. A sociable man, he dies, among his Bajan kin, aged forty-four.

HEREDITY

The gold buttons on Mr Bull's blazer have worn
away to silver. One of 'the new men', he's been
spotted popping in The Mason's Arms at lunchtime,
for two pork pies and three pints of lager-and-lime,
with Mr Speer, the Deputy Head. 'Bully' dubs
us 'yobbos', has a 'tache like Graham Souness's
and frequently plimsolls first-years' arses.

He claims today's double Biology will be 'fun';
as much so as the lesson when Ronnie Ruff swung
his Gola holdall onto his shoulder, shattering,
as he did so, a glass tank chocker with mating
locusts, who seized the moment to leap, still coupled,
to the darkest corners of the lab, while the whole
class shrieked. The memory of it makes Bully scowl.

He wonders who can roll their tongues – all of us.
His next test is notably tougher: wiggling ears.
Only little Steven Chivers sticks up his hand.
He says it's a gift inherited from his nan:
first his left lughole quivers, then his right; and then
both; a euphony of effortful rotation.
But it's not his ears that crack us up – it's the motion

of his outsized eyebrows, waltzing across his face.

NUMANOID

'I'll be loving you always,' croons Groucho, one of two African Greys brought back in his Merchant Navy heyday by Mr Paine, against whom I play a weekly and all but wordless game of chess. Groucho's cage-mate, Chico, munching pumpkin seeds while hanging upside down, wolf-whistles with fraternal derision as Groucho continues his repertoire of clicks, show-tune trills and a cocky 'Hello ladies'.

My brother Andy and I watch the summer's final test; or, rather, highlights of a match from the '76 series, shoved into the schedule to fill the rain-interrupted afternoon session once gusty Peter West has run out of talking-points and old pros to mull them over with. Just as the highlights come to their climax, they suddenly stop, because the umpires at The Oval are walking out again.

A siren mews louder and louder, until an ambulance arrives next door. Ten minutes later, when the message filters round that poor old Mr Paine – for years having lived in sin with Miss Peach – has succumbed to a stroke, we're in the garden: I'm slouching sunwards in a deck-chair and Andy's stretching out on the lounger, singing loudly along to his portable radio's thrum: 'And I die, you die.'

KING FOR A DAY

No-one could've been more surprised than Tim
to find himself at the apex
of a motorcycle formation team,

a perfect pyramid of human bricks
proceeding along the High Road
past the soon-to-be pulverised gasworks

where, this glorious Good Friday, a crowd
frenziedly applauds Tim's chutzpah
for standing in for the usual hothead.

Tim wishes he hadn't worn a jumper
beneath the petrol-blue leathers
because his sweat is rendering him damper

than an up-ending pintail's feathers.
Now he's stretching out his arms
like Jesus, a care-free sign that gathers

the approbation of the patriarchs
leaving St Joseph's in the sun,
while the magically balanced team makes

its way to the Guildhall, where everyone
related to them congregates
with hooters and banners and everything –
and Tim's coronation awaits.

FIRST DIGS

Mrs McCall's four-storey end-of-terrace, by a wall of biblical verse,
contained an oblique Atlantic view, of three of the Skerries, in whose
shelter long freighters dropped anchor. Goldfish foraged a plant-less
habitat in the hallway tank. The toffee-glossed walls of the staircase

to our separate accommodation were hung with royalist memorabilia,
crowned by one of those Fifties, Cecil Beaton, Kodacolor-*cum*-sepia
snaps of the 'grand' Queen Mum, whose dark-blue Order of the Garter
cloak had an oily, beguiling depth. Mrs McCall's nameless terrier's

fly-black nose was shoved into the shits it left on the living-room rug.
It blazed its anger from the family kitchen, whilst we, in ours, rubbed
along: Boyd, from the arch-Loyalist Ballybeen Estate, Dundonald, dug
all shades of Dylan, and kindly took my English accent down the pub,

after which he pulled off his party piece – of shinning up a lamp-post
like St Symeon Stylites; and Sinéad, all flame-maned rage, taught us
a whole new litany of usages for 'fuck', and put a good few into use
the time that Mrs McCall played 'God Save the Queen' at breakfast.

One November night, Barbara-Ann, Mrs McCall's blonde twin sister,
lurched up in pyjamas to our landing and pestered anyone to kiss her.
I gorged on Malcolm Lowry's stories of the sea. My bedroom's vista
was far from oceanic. But I was at large in the world; at last a 'Mister'.

ISOSCELES

Where courting oystercatchers make landfall,
Head-the-Ball won't walk the triangle's short side,
from Portstewart to Portrush: Satan would suck
his soul and toss him in the ocean 'like a stone'.

Instead, he negotiates the equal sides: down
to Coleraine then up Atlantic Road to Portrush,
where he bears away from the headland headwinds,
pitches his mast—legs into Paul's Bar's downstairs,
and openly adds to his rust-red pint of Smithwick's
a more-than-generous nip of hip-flask poteen.

Flogging downers to students and the desperate,
he recollects at length about his 'previous life',
Prohibition-busting in Al Capone's gang –
'I was in Chicago . . .' He stops mid-anecdote,
knocks back his drink, steers for the doors
and clomps the two long sides of the triangle home.

KINGSTON

So I hitched to see my folks in the Smoke;
first in a Monaghan Mushrooms lorry,
which fetched me up to Larne for the ferry.
It was rough. As the pipers from Ulster's
maddest kick-the-Pope band started to boke
overboard, I roared to myself in the bar.

In Stranraer, I thumbed a ride straightaway,
from a Geordie priest, who asked if I prayed:
I told him no, but he dropped me at Scotch
Corner anyhow. Then a brand-new Porsche
Carrera stopped: I blathered to the bloke
else his eyes would've closed and we'd've croaked.

At the next services, a campervan
espied my scrawled-on-cardboard 'London' sign.
I partied hard with four other hitchers
in the back, who smelled like they were fixtures
on the road, endlessly smoking the path
down south, and back to the Madchester north.

Near Toddington, I changed the sign to 'Heathrow'.
A white-van man headed toward Sipson
looked bemused that I was bound for Kingston,
and as we approached the airport's limits,
he warily enquired, in mellow
Cockney, 'Kingston's in Jamaica, innit?'

PIETÀ

After necking
a quick quartet of pints
consisting of two-thirds Guinness
and one-third special-offer just-out-of-date Gold Label barley wine,
Mervyn knocked back *con brio* a trio of double brandies;

        and now,

wearing only snug white y-fronts
in our flat above his, stociously bogarts a joint;

        regurgitates

the instant during a mushroom trip
one post-pub evening the previous Easter when
two IRA volunteers – students, it transpired –

        opened fire and shot

a pair of RUC reservists
who regularly stood on foot patrol
in the spot where they fell
outside Sportsland amusements, Main Street;

        and how

as the younger and sexier policeman died
he did so in the grip of Mervyn's muscular arms,
shrilling
like the lifeboat-siren's roar
for the whole cold port and hinterland to hear.

DUCKWALKING IN WEST BERLIN

Wangling a week's work with Teale's, who garden the British Sector quarters,
I'm assigned to learn the basics from Terry, who's been at it for years:
coining it in from the Federal Government's social generosity,
whilst earning a big enough wedge each summer to winter in Bali.

Last evening, Terry saw Miles Davis play his new album, *Tutu*,
and Chuck Berry, 'the best-ever support act', duckwalk 'like a nutter'.
Terry re-enacts the walk across the flowerbeds: head nodding forth
like a mid-river moorhen's; sunburnt kneecaps raking the bone-dry earth.

Later, I'm paired for weeding with Basildon Baz, at what he insists
was Eva Braun's house. After a lazy hour, we share a few spliffs
and dawdle round to sightsee the DDR wall guards, no older than
me, pacing up and down like the polar bears in the Tiergarten sun.

Baz and I degrade them further by mooning our Neo-Liberal arses;
as Rudolf Hess hangs himself in Spandau, inducing tanked-up Nazis
to bellow 'Horst Wessel' and slam along the towpath in Neukölln,
not sufficiently hammered yet to goose-step with total abandon.

THE GREAT STORM

So the three of us – Kevin, Mike and I –
are sat there like Compo, Foggy and Clegg,
sharing a joint and genial nonsense, on the trunk
of a storm-wrenched oak between Gallows Pond
and the sugar-maple plantation starting to turn.

Mike relates what happened when the storm
arrived, just after our mate Dave's stag do:
he got home to the flat he shared with the frontman
of a soon-to-be seminal prog–punk band,
guzzled a mugful of magic mushroom tea

and came up to Foetus and The Fall;
wandered the wind-fisted streets, taking/not-taking
everything in – the lampposts snapped
at ninety degrees, fences wrecked
like a set of smashed-in teeth, road-signs

pointing in the wrong direction as if the War
were still on – until he finally returned
hours later, to gurn in alarmed delight
as his front-door key drooped before the lock,
like a candle melting back into itself.

DONNY GILLIGAN THE LAB TECHNICIAN

tips up at 10 for tea and custard creams
in the admin. hub with Eileen and me.
His smile's as broad and deep as the Bann,
curving out of Coleraine toward the sea.

Donny tells us how he skippered a boat
that fished every day off Rathlin Island
for pollack and spurdog, wrasse and conger;
with a sideline smuggling hash from Scotland.

Kneecapped for his crime, he scarpered, and tripped
on acid in Amsterdam: his brain froze
when he manoeuvred a wheelchair in front
of Vincent's whirligig *Wheatfield with Crows*.

Donny maintains his night-time vision's
twenty–twenty because of ganja, like
Jamaican fishermen who artfully steer
between rocks in the Caribbean dark.

When he dreams, it's always of his future,
spliffed up in a Castlerock cul-de-sac –
with kerbstones painted marijuana green,
sun yellow, Red Leb red and Afghan black.

'Wanna blast?' he whispers. On some pretext,
I follow Donny to the lab. I lock
the door and he fires up the hubbly-
bubbly he's configured to cool the smoke:

long glass tube, water-filled bowl, valve and hose.
The whole Heath Robinson contraption sings
in gurgles. Donny draws like he's drinking
a milkshake through a straw, filling his lungs.

Before we know it, we're as merrily
wrecked as Cheech and Chong. We snigger and lurch
back down to finish our tea. Eileen's
busy, copying hymn-sheets for her church.

RASHARKIN

i.m. Karen Donovan

A vat of vile psychedelic tea
is stirred every now and then by Perky,

the chirpiest Hell's Angel you could meet,
whose drollery chunters right up your street,

his Ballymoney accent teetering
on your ear, an uncle balladeering.

A mugful of tea and you're well away,
driving your Metro like there's no today:

a game of dodge-the-river-bridge-roadblock.
You follow labyrinthine back-roads back,

like Pacman reversing into twilight.
The rose moon rises in the harvest night.

POSTCARDS TO PORT

Karachi, wasn't it, from where you sent the first one?
Wherever, whenever, all we knew was: travelling
was wholly wasted on you. We would've profited
so very much more. Why did you go there anyway?
You wrote some old cobblers about 'working your passage'
on a tanker sailing from Rotterdam, for scrapping
in the yard at Gadani, where old ships go to die.

Then another card arrived, from Assam: you'd swallowed
too much, too spicy, too soon; and were laid-up for weeks
on a Himalayan tea-plantation, with thinking-
time between fevers. Why were we not surprised to hear
that you went on to hire two rugby XVs'-worth
of Sherpas to bear you up Everest *umpteen* times?
Regale us now with the fine points of all your climbs.

SENSATIONAL HUMAN CANNONBALL

Before a suitably sloshed
 and pilled-up crowd
  on the headland hill
   above the harbour –
    which has already been thrilled
     by a Kiwi escapologist
      taking three minutes longer
       than the five allotted
        by the Yorkshire MC
         to emerge from a straitjacket,
          padlocked chains
           and flaming turps-doused box –
            the Human Cannonball rockets out,
             golden-helmeted,
              rainbowed in satin;
               a gust-propelled woodpigeon
                clattering wings
                 through the purpled evening sky;
                  to arch one hundred and fifty feet,
                   like a lovers' leap,
                    a constellation of sequins,
                     into the beckoning quayside net.

3

SCARECROW

Charles Paul, Aged Ten, 1872

St Swithun's Day dawn. A goshawk
fossicks the fields of Combe Hill Farm.
All the crows and jackdaws have flown.
Charley drowses within the corn,
though woe betide if Master Buss,
the headman, should witness him so.

Charley can read and write; will soon
become a journeyman butcher
in Eastbourne, wed, like his parents,
at the Zoar Strict Baptist Chapel,
Lower Dicker, then propagate
roses and seven fine children.

Now, he scares a ten-hour day,
for a shilling sixpence per week,
swivelling the rat-a-tat clapper
over his head, like the Zulu
chieftains brandishing assegais
in *Illustrated London News*.

THE SLEEPER

For this assignment, he'd been questioned by old-boy spooks:
'Are you a Red?' Well, he takes *The Guardian*, but mainly
for the cryptic crossword, cricket coverage and the font.
At Inverness, he boards the Far North train to Thurso,
pulls tight shut the thick ex-LNER green curtains
to keep out a glint of the midsummer all-night sun
which bathes the Strath of Kildonan's pines and gold on this
last leg of the twelve-hour trip from London to Caithness,
where blackcocks *lek* and Risso's dolphins leap.

He wolfs a breakfast of smokies, then it's access-all-
areas at Dounreay. To bleary eyes, the 'golf ball'
fast reactor looks more like a ping-pong ball. Munro,
the deputy manager, has been expecting him –
no spot-checks permitted at the edge of the Free World.
Shielded by overalls and rubber gloves, he records
the rod-backed delight with which Munro depicts morale
within the busiest workforce, by far, in Caithness,
where blackcocks *lek* and Risso's dolphins leap.

He finds no fault, beyond the idiocy of 'boffins'
sent up from Hinkley Point to boost productivity.
After he's chosen presents for home and single malts
for himself, there's barely time to glimpse the local sights,
like Scrabster harbour, where whitefish trawlers are anchored.
But as he settles on the train, he ponders his purpose
as 'the Man from Whitehall', and dreams of hermitage and rest,
and little to do except lighten up, in Caithness,
where blackcocks *lek* and Risso's dolphins leap.

VINYL

The beechwood radiogram stood right here.
It held Mum's clutch of records, from before
their wedding, on Hitler's birthday, sadly –
South Pacific, 'Blow the Wind Southerly',
Nat King Cole . . . And Dad's, all bought years later:
Western themes, James Last and His Orchestra,
the Band of the Coldstream Guards, Herb Alpert
and the Tijuana Brass, Bert Kaempfert . . .

Despite the stylus jumping in the groove,
I repeatedly played at forty-five
my coloured-vinyl singles. To *start* with;
then every available speed. The sloth
of thirty-three. Seventy-eight: dirty,
psychotic, punked-up Pinky and Perky.
Sixteen was by far the most alluring –
like savagely pissed-up ogres slurring.

SUNDAY AT THE OVAL WITH DAD

We hear it coming. A hullabaloo
at the Vauxhall End hoorays into view
as a Mexican wave. Where we're sitting,
in the Pavilion's top tier, tutting
from 'the panamas' morphs into bathos
as the wave surfs anti-clockwise across
the West Stand. I can almost touch the qualm
becoming sweat that Dad exhales from
intrinsic dread at the thought of joining
in. But he mustn't do disappointing.
Tanned to teak, he tips his sun-hat aslant,
drops the pencil, and for just that moment
mercurially resolves to live ad hoc:
we throw our arms right up to twelve o'clock.

HEADGEAR

Granddad bought this brown-banded panama
in a family-run department store in Eastbourne,
having cussedly tried on hat after hat after hat
that hot and jaunty afternoon; then wore it
to change the flowers at my grandma's grave.

The hat's among others in the cupboard:
the white-paint-splattered, navy-blue beret
that Dad used to wear while decorating;
and a bobble hat knitted by Mum which kept
his slicked-back, jet-black hair in place

after washing it, an hour until bedtime,
the radio talking, radiators on full blast,
before he inventorially double-locked
the front door, then the back door,
and turned off all the lights.

THE SIDECAR

Dad affixed 'the egg' to his BSA 600 side valve:
no more weaving between traffic lanes
like next door's tomcat squeezing through the fence.

After their first spin, from Mill Hill to Staples Corner,
Mum laughed, 'It's just like a dodgem.'
Samuel slept on her lap throughout the trip

until he woke at lights, bushbaby-eyed and babbly,
as if the speed and vivacity were exactly why
he'd been forceped into the family.

Dad recollects those times with eyelids shut:
each wheezy kick-start and low, grunting rev
makes the lucent white of his memory run.

BRITISH SUMMER TIME'S END

As Dad lolls down in the care-home armchair,
cleft double chin almost touching his shirt,
I ease him upright and, for what it's worth,

unstrap his watch to wind it back an hour:
that Dad no longer knows the day, the month
or year is probably neither here nor there.

An un-drunk milky tea squats on a plate.
'I was a crack shot; especially at
the Bren, but it was much too accurate.'

By night, he gets half-dressed for going out:
'To interrogate a Russian spy, caught
red-handed with a nuclear secret.'

I ask him if he'll eat his slice of cake.
'I'm off to the school to teach them to waltz.'
The lead clinician laughs for laughter's sake.

THE D WORD

Dad's been disturbing other patients by yelling, so now has a side-room to himself. He's demeaned by 'safety mittens', the big white boxing gloves he sports to prevent him pulling out the lines from the cannula. The doctors were supposed to gain my consent, but how could I refuse? None is fully qualified yet; nonetheless, each volunteers the corporate prognosis with vigorous compassion.

As I say hello, Dad further closes his eyes, to exclude my voice, as though he's wearing headphones from his just-retired, Hawaiian-shirt years. I ask him how he's feeling, without response. I witter on about work, the kids, and how Mum promises to visit as soon as she's mobile. Just when Dad appears preoccupied by matters in another time and place, he murmurs, 'Are you here *again*?'

I marvel at the view from this sixth floor of Twickenham Wing: south-west London *haka*s in the face of north-east Surrey. 'Come on', barks Dad. 'Where to?' I ask. 'Come *on!*' he insists. Is he calling Andy and me when we were kids, dawdling half a road behind him on the way to the cricket? Or Jigsaw, our family cat, perhaps, hesitant on the back step at the sight of drizzle? Or death itself?

THE SEWING KIT

A fortnight after my father's death,
Mum recounts the details of my birth:

how my brothers, aged seven and four,
waited for news on the bottom stair,

as Dad raced round to the surgery –
doubtlessly swearing like buggery –

to fetch the RAF sewing kit
that Dr Cox, in his haste, forgot;

and on my delivery, Cox, dad
of three young boys himself, exclaimed, 'Snap!'

As he sewed her up afterwards, Cox
told my mother he'd embroidered ducks.

QUEEN QUEENIE

After the storm subsides, you find
your glass garden table in smithereens,
kites of plane-leaves sprawling over the fence,
and the closest to silence you've ever heard outdoors.
You're alive as the young cat who appears once a week,
her eyes like a frog's peeping out from the pond
your neighbours say you must get filled in.

But as another dreary year accumulates,
like autumn's rain within a cracked terracotta pot,
you hear instead the last few blackberries –
for bramble jelly, crumbles and fools –
still singing lustily on their bush.

NOTES

Several poems in this collection stem from Pascale Petit's 'Poetry from Art' sessions at Tate Modern and Tate Britain, between 2008 and 2013. Of those poems, only 'High Wire' and 'Juniper Child' are more direct, rather than tangential, responses to artworks: Catherine Yass's 2008 video 'High Wire' and Joan Jonas's 1976 installation 'The Juniper Tree' (reconstructed in 1994) respectively.

'Hop Picking' – Prompted by some incidents in *East Sussex Within Living Memory*, East Sussex Federation of Women's Institutes, 1995.

'Mrs Peabody' – I am indebted to Andrea Robinson for kindly allowing me to use an anecdote of hers for the basis of this poem.

'The Stones at Redlands' – Prompted by an anecdote of Mick Jagger's in Brett Morgen's 2012 documentary film *Crossfire Hurricane*.

'The Chimps' – Lizzie Dripping was the eponymous hero of Helen Cresswell's mid-1970s children's books and BBC television series.

'The Triumph of Sylvester Clarke' – The match, played at The Oval, was a Nat West Trophy semi-final which was rain-interrupted and therefore played over two days.

'Numanoid' – Gary Numan's 'I Die, You Die' peaked at number 6 in the UK singles chart in August 1980.

'Scarecrow' — Prompted by a snippet about his father in the unpublished memoirs of my grandfather, WRH Paul.

'Sunday at the Oval with Dad' — 'the panamas' refers to the crustier Surrey County Cricket Club members who disapproved of Mexican waves.

ACKNOWLEDGEMENTS

Thanks are due to the editors and publishers of the following publications/websites where some of these poems, or previous versions, first appeared: *The Best New British and Irish Poetry 2016*, Eyewear Publishing, 2016; *The Best New British and Irish Poetry 2017*, Eyewear Publishing, 2017; *Blowing Raspberries*; *Butcher's Dog*; *Contemporary Haibun 15*, Red Moon Press, 2014; *Contemporary Haibun Online*; *Football Poets*; *Good Dadhood*; *Ink, Sweat and Tears*; *Magma*; *Nth Position*; *Poetry from Art at Tate*, Tate, 2011; *The Rialto*; *Simply Haiku*; the Tate Modern website; and *The Wardrobe*.

Some of these poems were included within a short collection which was shortlisted for the Poetry School/Pighog Press pamphlet competition 2013.

'Numanoid' was long-listed for the National Poetry Competition 2013.

Thanks for their invaluable help and encouragement are due to the following: Katherine Gallagher, Hamish Ironside, Roy Kelly, Adrian Paul, Lyn Paul, Pascale Petit, Clare Pollard, Ann Sansom, Peter Sansom, and the Red Door Poets – Hanne Busck-Nielsen, Tom Cunliffe, Beatríz Echeverri, Katie Griffiths, Chris Hardy, Elizabeth Horsley, Gillie Robic and MJ Whistler. Special thanks to Todd Swift, Rosanna Hildyard and the rest of the Eyewear team.

⌐◡⌐ **EYEWEAR** PUBLISHING

EYEWEAR'S TITLES INCLUDE

EYEWEAR
POETRY

ELSPETH SMITH DANGEROUS CAKES
CALEB KLACES BOTTLED AIR
GEORGE ELLIOTT CLARKE ILLICIT SONNETS
HANS VAN DE WAARSENBURG THE PAST IS NEVER DEAD
BARBARA MARSH TO THE BONEYARD
DON SHARE UNION
SHEILA HILLIER HOTEL MOONMILK
MARION MCCREADY TREE LANGUAGE
SJ FOWLER THE ROTTWEILER'S GUIDE TO THE DOG OWNER
AGNIESZKA STUDZINSKA WHAT THINGS ARE
JEMMA BORG THE ILLUMINATED WORLD
KEIRAN GODDARD FOR THE CHORUS
COLETTE SENSIER SKINLESS
ANDREW SHIELDS THOMAS HARDY LISTENS TO LOUIS ARMSTRONG
JAN OWEN THE OFFHAND ANGEL
A.K. BLAKEMORE HUMBERT SUMMER
SEAN SINGER HONEY & SMOKE
HESTER KNIBBE HUNGERPOTS
MEL PRYOR SMALL NUCLEAR FAMILY
ELSPETH SMITH KEEPING BUSY
TONY CHAN FOUR POINTS FOURTEEN LINES
MARIA APICHELLA PSALMODY
TERESE SVOBODA PROFESSOR HARRIMAN'S STEAM AIR-SHIP
ALICE ANDERSON THE WATERMARK
BEN PARKER THE AMAZING LOST MAN
ISABEL ROGERS DON'T ASK
REBECCA GAYLE HOWELL AMERICAN PURGATORY
MARION MCCREADY MADAME ECOSSE
MARIELA GRIFFOR DECLASSIFIED
MARK YAKICH THE DANGEROUS BOOK OF POETRY FOR PLANES
HASSAN MELEHY A MODEST APOCALYPSE
KATE NOAKES PARIS, STAGE LEFT
JASON LEE BURNING BOX
U.S. DHUGA THE SIGHT OF A GOOSE GOING BAREFOOT
TERENCE TILLER THE COLLECTED POEMS
MATTHEW STEWART THE KNIVES OF VILLALEJO
PAUL MULDOON SADIE AND THE SADISTS
JENNA CLAKE FORTUNE COOKIE
TARA SKURTU THE AMOEBA GAME
MANDY KAHN GLENN GOULD'S CHAIR
CAL FREEMAN FIGHT SONGS
TIM DOOLEY WEEMOED
MATTHEW PAUL THE EVENING ENTERTAINMENT